SOUL IN SPACE

PUBLISHED BY WAVE BOOKS

WWW.WAVEPOETRY.COM

COPYRIGHT © 2013 BY NOELLE KOCOT

ALL RIGHTS RESERVED

WAVE BOOKS TITLES ARE DISTRIBUTED TO THE TRADE BY

CONSORTIUM BOOK SALES AND DISTRIBUTION

PHONE: 800-283-3572 / SAN 631-760X

THIS TITLE IS AVAILABLE IN LIMITED EDITION HARDCOVER

DIRECTLY FROM THE PUBLISHER

LIBRARY OF CONGRESS CATALOGING-IN-PUBLICATION DATA

KOCOT, NOELLE.

[POEMS. SELECTIONS]

SOUL IN SPACE / NOELLE KOCOT.—FIRST EDITION.

PAGES CM

ISBN 978-1-933517-74-2 (ALK. PAPER)

ISBN 978-1-933517-79-7 (LIMITED EDITION HARD COVER)

I. TITLE.

PS3611.O36S68 2013

811'.6—DC23

2012046701

DESIGNED AND COMPOSED BY QUEMADURA

PRINTED IN THE UNITED STATES OF AMERICA

9 8 7 6 5 4 3 2 1

FIRST EDITION

WAVE BOOKS 039

FOR MY MOTHER, JO-ANN SLEIGHT

CONTENTS

I

II

IV

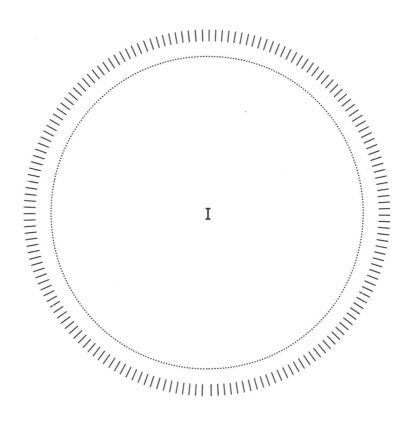

I

TALK

My body is
A little
Green sea.

Bears bathe
In it
Then go to

Sleep in the
Basement.
A four-wheeler

Slams past,
And then the
Sea splashes

Around and
Around.
O little sea,

O my body,
Sit here with me
While I just talk.

I light the sky
With streamers and bandannas!

The storm is beautiful!
I run around in it,

Taste the water on
My mouth.

How many days and nights
Will haunt us, here,

In this place?
The storm.

Mine and mine to keep
In the palm of my aching hand.

APRIL IN NEW JERSEY

We vaguely escaped
From the rhododendron,

When the ant
Crossed your knee.

The foothills rang.
The sun gleamed.

A few horses broke
Away

And went somewhere
That started with a C.

Simple delight came
Down like a runny

Nostril. Fences of
Silver kept us in,

Forever? No, just
Until lunchtime

When we would
Be unfit for feeling.

SPIRIT

Whadja say? How be it
In the murk.

But no, gone now,
And the birds

Dance on thick wrists.
Love, love

To all, in this sunny
Season.

The watches have stopped,
The spirit goes.

ABODE

The only branches,
The wind just about

Broke them,
The limbs bending

Forward.
It's the way things heave

In the sunlight.
A woman fans herself.

So what? It is her
Abode.

Tumbling at the edge
Of disaster,

This is how I lived.
Oh see how the chrysanthemums

Are dry now,
Yet still beautiful.

Here is something
For the ages,
A turn in the heavens
Which will bring us
Forward.
Dark as day
We go,
Face of unsuspecting stone
Hammered out
And spread
Like a willow
Over the land.

NIGHT ARBOREAL

Talk & laughter in the faded rooms.
Oh, when will we see each other?

In the lemon day that hangs
Overhead,

I will go and find a draped
Lunatic and say, "This is my golden,

Golden." Bartering means,
I do not wish to be left alone.

Or, yes, it's okay to now be left alone.

Rising shoots of tombstones:
Chiseled buds reaching
Toward a flesh-toned moon.

THE 4TH DAY AFTER
QUITTING CIGARETTES

The sun rises, too,
Over my water-
Logged heart.

Baskets full of hymns,
The streaming light

Over these branches
Unseen. Wild over.

The wind sanctifies
The old,

The downtrodden verbs
Which direct you

To a place where all things
Live.

Mouth running over us
In a cold stream.

The beauty of it?
The -ied.

All fire and wisp
Beyond which

The rain directly
Waits.

Winter churches
Call,

From where, we
Do not yet know.

If I could unravel
You

Into a pound of
Bread,

The sea would
Lay its version

Of flax upon
Your hair.

A heartless spirit.
Nowhere near

The sea.

LIGETI

The curse of the fathers. The
Good gifts. Now you want to

Mess it all up. The orange
Orange. The movement of

Grace beneath you runs like
An Orphic vision. Your wild

Pulse, what does it affirm?
Ask by implication, ask by gesture.

Don't touch me, I'm alive.

ON THE DEBUT OF OLIVIER MESSIAEN'S
QUARTET FOR THE END OF TIME

30,000 _____ poke their heads
Above the Görlitz snow.

A snap-stringed cello tautens
The air to a wire.

Somewhere an angel has counted
Infinity wrong, and rests his cheek
Upon the stars.

E . S . T .

Noon
Spinning in our eyes like coins.

1 p.m.
The sleepy dangers

2 p.m.
The rest of the pie

3 p.m.
Eye of the haystack

4 p.m.
Buildings swaying in wind

5 p.m.
Steak without onions

6 p.m.
Onions

7 p.m.

Loose threads on the beds

8 p.m.

Long shadows

9 p.m.

The cat chases the light

10 p.m.

Church bells

11 p.m.

Life everlasting

Midnight

We catch the musk

1 a.m.

Letting go of all preconceptions

2 a.m.

We sleep alone

3 a.m.

Our pagan friends

4 a.m.

Hour of the wolf

5 a.m.

Another country wakes

6 a.m.

Coffee-stained fingers

7 a.m.

Love for all things

8 a.m.

Overdrive

9 a.m.

A little music?

10 a.m.

Turkeys eat their feed

11 a.m.

There is a first time and an end time. Choose.

I'm going to make this my thing,
That's right. On a sundial,

I travel aisles of chrysanthemums.
Morning huddles around the hosts

Of wanting, as if you recalled a
Darker day, rumbling the depths

Of psychotic beauty, while I try
To make sense of you, poem,

Poem, in the disturbed valencies
Of wind. Here the water drips

Sound into meaning. Here I can
Weep my fill about everything.

POEM FOR NEW JERSEY

These mellow streets, this corn,
This golden rain,

Even the stray dogs have their say.
Thursday is a leaf

Falling out of the mouth.
Doped to sleep on reference,

We dream of the Hanover Salon.
The landscape has been

With me for a lifetime now.
New Jersey, you have blown into

My room so imperceptibly,
And there is no lack of tenderness

In my address.
Heal me, and I will make you a tree

Out of pagodas, or a pagoda out
Of a tree, or a dog

That sits waiting for a bookstore
On which to be leashed forever.

The way things intersect
Underneath the foggy trees.

The way there is no moon
Today, the way hurt

Blossoms. Go out and fetch
The milk pail,

The mailbox is waiting
For its wreath.

Climb out against the seedlings,
Look to where the bridges meet.

If I bent down and touched
The timber of your knees . . .

That's all I got. Transcendence
Seems ugly. Puerile, like wishing

On a traffic light. Or, wanting a
Reward. Wanting the cat who is

Always hungry. Give it a rest.
The streets are clean and

Shiny without me, and the blood
Flows just like blood.

Birds chirp over me,
Too early for them and yet.
My mind is not right.

The thickening haze of
Cigarette smoke can do wonders
For a private eyesore.

Jump like a lamb into the void.
Teach me all that is unsaid,
Because I want to hear it,

And because I left without knowing.

HOW I KNOW I AM
NOT REALLY LIVING

Exodus, omens, premonitions, bluest
Electricity ambling down a wire.

When darkness falls, the scent of wood
Is strong. The deer has shed its antlers.

The feeling of labor turns orange in the dusk.
A bug of light in the detritus flies away.

The starlit leaves on a mountain—
The house is bare. The cupboards
Are bare. And who is to say I am
Not totally alone anymore, wandering

The streets in my sleeves? I tell
You this: the longer you avoid me,
The longer you will not get to see
Yourself in my mirror, which is valuable

And good. Close your eyes. Go off
Somewhere in the deep night. The
Mountain is exploding now, and you
Are on top of it. I am at the bottom

Looking up at you. I see nothing at all.

Motherless skies about a planar moon.
I've had a new discovery today.

The lithesome flower that we did not pick
Grows spectacularly from a line.

There is no other growing here, no fauna,
No expectation of getting dressed so early anymore.

Leave the suitcases behind. Walk away
From it all. Remember to sell that little

Doll you had in its awakening. No number
Gives us comfort or beginnings. The

Quiet stars peek out from their small rooms.

Look at the landscape,
A lot of damage, no?
But we are here together,
And of needing me, where
The world needs me,
We are too alone.
And what of our orange daylight,
Growing darker as the lamplit
Trees grow darker. There
Is not enough to say.
But our hands, our gentle
Frozen hands sift through
Things like numbers out of breath.
It will all be okay, I promise.
Promise who? Promise the faded land.

Not the lemon-gold

On a spectral hillside. Not the fawning
Girls. Not the silos.

Yeah yeah yeah, but I'm serious.
I am just barely a pattern.

The elegant reduced to surf,
See the topography through the waves,

The cycles of births & deaths.
This feeling of being saved

I cannot shake tonight, the pure
On top of the pure stacked upon the pure.

Traffic lighter now than it was,
The sole survivor of yesterday's wreck

Always has more to say.

NUDE ANTS

Talking about oneself is rarely
Intimate. The birds fly off
Somewhere, the lichens follow.
There is something

So spontaneous and restorative
About a walk through a super-
Market at dusk. A little light
Peeks out from the cereal boxes,

The old ladies patiently await
Their turn. Ugliness: I I I.
But beauty is self-protective
Sometimes, and what is there

To do? Judge not these glistening
Towels of amber. Judge the
Circus-dry levees of a hundred
Wasted hydrants—oh music without

Rain, behind all this, some great
Happiness is hiding.

Not makeup, not a little distance,
Not the houses, the color of rose,

Not a spare tire around the waist,
Not the blue gates around the feral

Cats, not Macy's, not necromancy,
Not memory's glittering movement,

Not the ankle shoes, not the brilliant
Snowflakes over this rural suburb,

Nothing can keep me from getting
Into a taxi today, and riding off

Into my city. I am the lover and
The beloved, and I don't believe

That miracles happen without this
Hair and these sleeves, flowing like

The legs of passersby. The moment
Stands revised, and so does the

Accompaniment of illusion, radiance,
A stammering, late mosquito on the sill.

The will to make something beautiful
Out of nothing—two stars in the fury

Of the Big Bang. Nothing separates
From anything, the light breaks on

The keyboard, the anthills grow bigger,
The flowers open and open. I say,

Touch me, or let me touch you, in a
Garden filled with daylilies. The sun

Will also set, we will become specks
Like that in the dusk, crying to go home.

S.A.D.

This fall weather attacks me!
Vulnerable, cut open,

Head full of staples and straw.
Suicidally kind,

I enter through the narrow gate.
Then I turn back

To greet the xanthophyll sorrow
Splattering over the provocative

Wash of the day.

DREAM OF NYC

Excess of voice. Latitudes and longitudes
Of eternity. I am wine, and this my song.

I will incinerate precisely a fire engine
And some snow. Taxi? Where are you?

AFTER THE FEEDING

With the imaginary hand, I spoil
All of your drinking water. Poor
Soul, nothing can protect you.
Infinite thirst, come back and quote

The living. Enjoy yourself. Encourage
The memory of restoration. Locusts
Ate us, and then they stopped in their
Colorful tracks. I place a bracket

Around the midnight turkeys, lined
In a row, waiting for me to feed them.

SEAGULLS

Part-winged, the face of the shore
Expelled upon a shell.

This is what I call a wick
Of an expression.

This is what I call "intense."
It is getting misty out.

There is a group of crows, hovering.
What do you call those other birds?

Seagulls, Johnny, seagulls.

Poets are feral beasts.
They will not sleep
In the winter, they will
Not eat frozen foods.
The spring-sharp sky
Above them kills the
Ceiling. A slow, deliberate
Speaking through masks—
Uniqueness, nerve,
They love the woman
Called Dora in Freud.
Poets are beasts without
A reason—their poems
Are made into a little
Chapbook called Life
As Usual, and they want
To reach you, but don't.
The impact of waves,
A jar full of pennies,
The scissors lying open
On the ashes of the dead.
These things will not be

A Eureka, and everyone
Has gone to sleep. They wink
At the stars, and the purplest
Vessel shows that everyone
Above them is yearning.

HOME

And there you stood
In all of your leonine splendor.
I couldn't see you,
But I sensed you, right near
The vase of sunflowers.
You were looking at me.
You smiled, as only you could.
Ghost, I am in love with you,
And we are separate now,
Though you live inside me.
I never wanted us to be one,
But two, and this is how
The universe will have it.
Please know, I would never have
Forsaken you in life,
No matter what you did,
And I do not forsake you now,
On my own way back home.

POEM

With deepest reverence,
I shop for bones.

And what is the candy
And the daylight

And the horse without hunger?
Too many ducts for us to think of,

And here we are punishing the
Lines above our faces.

Enormity is a hoof
With unanswerable sounds,

And the void is filled with fire.
My dream is to fall apart,

To cry for a century,
But I have not cried, not at all.

I keep my distance like the tines
Of a fork from one another,

Dressing, undressing the fabulous wounds.
But now, back to our story,

It has coffee in it, a naked river.
Blessed are we who rapture

An electric wire, blessed be
The falling things about our faces,

Blessed is the socket of an eye
That lights the body, because

In the end, in the very end, it's
Just you. You and you. And you.

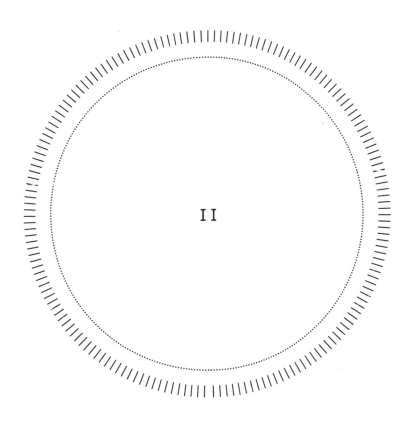

II

There it stood, naked and ashamed.

It looked into a surreal forest.

It listened to *La mer*.

It was austere in its way, like dandelions.

Unlike dandelions, it bled furies.

Like dandelions, it shed everything.

Whether it says, you're sick, go to the doctor,

Or whether it says, you're not sick, don't go to the doctor,

I will be mad.

I will be mad because it is my mother.

It screamed me into this world,

And I wish I had a sample of its handwriting

So that I would be less lonely.

It says, get some sleep

And so I sleep, and go somewhere warm

Where hell is an apple,

Neurons firing off without me,

Neurons that are a gift from long ago.

It doesn't laugh enough.

It doesn't eat enough.

It doesn't make a mess out of things.

It throws back its head and lets it bob like a big rubber ball.

It realizes everything too soon.

It doesn't wear dresses anymore.

It wears silver wrappings like a robot.

The world is its convent.

Its brothers and sisters are the trees.

It liked looking at pictures of cats
On the computer.

It was becoming that kind of person.

It lit a torch in the wind, and said,
How special.

It ate a lot of soup.

Of the interior life it said, "C'est la vie!"

Of the exterior, it wandered about, ageless
And far from home.

It liked reality almost as much as it liked the imagination.

It fed its ridiculous cat.

It went to work on a train shaped like a bee.

It had achieved greatness in its mind.

Its soul, however, rarely talked to anyone.

It mattered little which was its downfall.

It mattered little, but it mattered.

It filed away its disasters and threw away the key.

It kept itself very nice.

It looked into his eyes once and thought, save me

And he did.

Now there is only a distant birdsong in its ears.

It drove to a faraway place where there was no water.

It pardoned itself.

It genuflected to the curvature of the earth.

It sang songs about fish.

It wanted to be alone once and for all.

It winked at the hazel eye of the moon.

It is going on a long journey without socks.

It is a real lament in the daytime.

It likes to laze about and read short passages.

The tunnel of want is important to it.

It hardly ever blinks, and tears never fall from its dry eyes.

Its solar plexus is a knot of fear.

It loves to swim naked in the pouring rain.

It found itself in a cloud of gnats.

A blade of grass bounced in the wind.

It took pleasure in a girl's beauty.

A feast was held in its honor.

It ate and drank, but did not sing

For its sadness, which it confessed

To its brothers and sisters.

Yet it lives and moves and has its being.

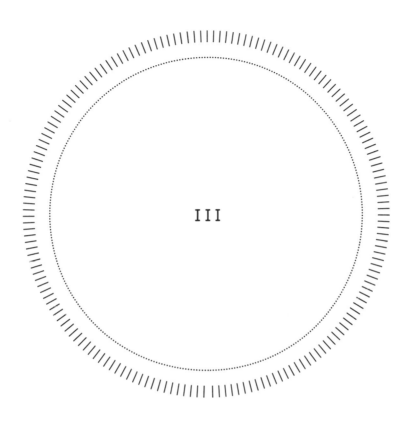

III

PRESENT

Love swept away the crumbs
And made its exit. Over the
Great fields of Horace, over the
Time-ridden monkey bars of yore,

There is a taking up of things.
The rambunctious night flutters
Like a towel, the past that makes us
Go around and around, it's how we

Have latched onto things. Beautiful
Stained glass surrounds me now.
I want nothing, and I want to give you
Nothing. This is why I say, hold

Me, as the many-limbed hunk of
Earth spins and spins, knocks us around.

THE SUPER-MEADOW

Now we have reached the super-meadow.
The long fat cows graze in the cool, tall grass.
The meadow is for their pleasure, not ours.
We like to go there when the day is thick

As soup, and we glean wild honey
From the hallowed ground. Super-meadow,
You are my friend, and I will always
Have a special place for you at Thanksgiving.

You will never be alone,
And you will never have to fight the fight
Of living, where the rest of the world
Will go by, combing its hair,

Sprinkling trails of entropy
On your weedless, wedless grass.

POOL SONNET

Lost was once one seen. Leaves tremble
In the background. Love is a vehicle of
Light, wheeling across the sentient grass.
Without me, who would suffer? I said

An age of things. Then, I backed away,
Went toward the world. The people looked
At me, naked, without a float on the water.
There was a tree—I ate of it, as we all

Would have. That's why there didn't need
To be any more tests. The light shone through
My chlorined hair. The smell was delicious,
And the mirror was fogged. A sandwich

Was there for us to munch on. Then, we drove
Off somewhere, I, them, and with each other.

BALLERINAS

A moth lamenting its wings, how
To worship? We are so famished,
Such a fantastic job on the ceilings
And the doors. Curtains, sky, the

Domesticated fog creeps over the
East. But here, we reach a different
Conclusion. Who is to invent the
Value of our soft caresses, who is to

Say who is missing? The waves
Misunderstood their dry sufferings.
The moated birds misheard their
Wingspans. A bitten moon hangs

Above winter. The little teeth of
Ballerinas keep us warm, full of life.

THE WARNING

If I have judged in some measure,
I will be judged in that measure.
Belly full of tacos, I hate it when Batman's
Voice gets so low. Does he think I'm

Stupid? To love the gold is to deny the spirit.
Many calves walk about the rooms.
If I should say, I will be increased, can I
Do it without throwing good wheat in the fire?

Love and song. Love and song. And now
I covet a star in the sky. There is no hope
For me it seems, but there is hope for you,
Hence I warn you: do not go where the

Cattle lay by themselves. Go into another night,
Filled with jasmine, myrrh and darkest sage.

THE DUCK

The war craft of seasons, the emergency in
The stream, no, we haven't mentioned the shock
Of the hospitable. Bundled down into our tensile
Calves, we see the hushed crowd of ancestors

Forming a line. In this case, we disappear. I
Am president of this town. I stopped in front
Of a puppy lying on the grass. Saliva dripped
From my mouth, and who is to say the origami

Duck I made will not fly? The black night sky
Over us, the flames spreading linen in the
Fields, a mine shaft waits for us to greet it, to ring
In the year with dozens of dead birds. Once, I was

Somewhere. Once the pedestrians looked at me
As I passed. My life is cooler now, more generous.

UNCIRCUMSCRIBED

The violet revolution, the way things swing
In the wind, the glittering parataxis when I
Speak of you. The plight of a cyclic revealingness
We might call irrational and yet. In the stillness,

Something is reclaimed. My brother, the metal
Voice lost in what goes through is our beforelight
That rings through the night. Epicene rigor—
I've spoken about it. The roar of enigma, the

Special volume on the other side of things, I
Fall to the inaudible ground. These edges surge
Blue and purple, these faces and their beauty
Go on laughing. What is shaped simply disappears.

I am not finished emptying myself, even though
I thought I was. Come here, see where the face is hidden.

HOUSEWARMING

I've lost sight of you, smothered serenade.
The night is a candy dish, perfumed by
Shadows. The heart burns with the mouth's
Light. On the backbone of ambiguity stands

A pale body. The heart keeps beating,
The lungs drown in inherent symmetry.
I miss the salt that pours out of my wounds,
I miss the apology, inherent in the air around

Them. I brought us here, in the twilit
Collateral, architecture on its head. A common
Name is like a chord looking through a camera.
At what? The humming in the wind

As you step, or suddenly tumble, what else
Is there to know? A liar singing to the grass.

REVERENCE IS OURS

Heaven in a ditch, the circle of little angels.
The future is a wound, the dissonant rev
Of whirling sentences. Your falsetto is alive
In these woodland wells, and this shine

Is more tribal melody than instrument.
Oh, you who have a watery sympathy with
Dirt, oh you mud and sticks and crawly
Things, the room is wandering on its depths,

You live in a flock of time, alive in that mirror.
The silence of the day is for exploring,
And your fever is an object. What do you have?
Stay home and smoke pipes. The whole continent

Is being tugged at. When did it last rain?
The lane is ending and there are no signs.

AS BLOSSOMS FALL

Tautened in the day's cares, the serenade
Drifts nobly on. We hold the ocean in our
Hands, we sing of lizards in the sand. An
Elixir that means beautiful, the wonderment

Is ours. Before the gestures, I can feel you
In my body, as you take me by the throat. The
Ambiguity of pets, the tongues of hours,
What remains is simply the crossing of the

Body's pillows. The quilts are all messed up,
The traffic is so late today. The peripatetic X
Marks its course like a coffee ring, a dog
In the street as the street goes dark. The looking

Glass beneath the mist is painted with decay.
An antidote to water resounds as blossoms fall.

CIRCULAR

The autumn breezes and the breezes' pain.
Not to comprehend that which pierced my
Gills, not to mention the shadow-light on
The walls that hold me up, it's because I have

Begun to peel my petals, the exhausted thirst
My hunger will devour. I am touching the
Whitened sky. There. Now I have got a dream
That fades into reality, the colleague of my

Wizened fingertips unspreading. Life of labor
Lit with a drowsy notion, I play knock-knock
Jokes on my earthly haven. Things
Stomp around grandiosely, a new layer of

Inconsolable suffering that meets the threshold
Of what eats this chorus around the moon that glows.

The whole world's machinations blossom.
The gleams come over. You were such
A taker of the breeze's pain, you were
Alive, there in the town. Licensed light

Shone like a brandy flask, the rock that
Never ages or returns. This word from
Water, anticipation, a green sea. I took
You by the hand, I dropped a book on

Your bed. Beneath any washed skeleton,
Beneath the dark veils, I, too, announce
My dearest tricks. On the ledge, I will
Adjust myself. I cross myself again.

The earth is a duck, getting up without
Us. The earth is a white line, no sea.

WITHOUT OURSELVES

In the precarious wind, those who died freely
Awaken. They have bled to erase the fat
From the scalps of those rustling in the hills.
No one owns their physical body. No one.

Let there be sections of bronze across our tables.
Let the miscreants come and taste once and twice.
A golden bee flies off somewhere. This cake
Is meant for our common kingdom. The loss

Of a child is the worst, and yet, she is going
Through it. The leaves fall off, pendulous,
Platitudinous. A continuous impossibility
Is an island in an ocean of night. Come with

Me then, travel far and wide. The moans
From the house will lead us back without ourselves.

SOME TIME

Light on a casualty, these scenes do not afford
Us. Like saying, I will do more for less, like saying,
You are the grubber in the panty drawer. A diamond
Evening, an offense taken with blind eyes. The

Wooden slats are open to an old mattress and some
Metal rings. The squirrels are crying. We have
Stopped paying attention. To our right sits the
Fleshy lips. We look prepared for what may come,

But now we are looking into the air for a relic of
Something. Drenched, we seek an unappointed
Hour. You hold the window open for me to vomit
Out of. There, the monster is on the floor. In the

Tall grass overlooking the fog, there is a roll of
Duct tape, a metallic balloon twisting in the wind.

FORMALISM ON A SUNDAY AFTERNOON

FOR ANTHONY MCCANN

The wolf howled at the flock, linguistics
Didn't matter. I spout tubes today from
My head, the trees, leaves, all over the place.
Another blue valley in a starboard eye-socket,

A paper touch of something else. Cities and
Shrubs are another man's loneliness. Soil
Mixed with an electric flare, the fortuity
Of rising, gossip of hopefulness, suppleness of words.

You will seize us with your power, I say, to
A turnstile that flames all night. Past the candlewick
That curls into sleep, past the soul's liturgy,
I stay in a state of liquid and ablation,

Winter emptied of its limit like a pigment,
Summer that ends with a star rising somewhere.

I have not wasted my life. The subtle
Interference, filled with risk and bad
Feelings, was made to sail across.
It is a weird admixture, the pretense

Of valor, oh, should I call it mechanical,
Or should I wait here, the skin over
My being now healed? The world is
Angular. The world is covered in a

Softness. The dark soil is lit by a
Nine-light chandelier. I have planted
My suffering and left it. I trade my hope
For an expression of stars. The plants

Sing a ballad in the mud after a snow.
One piano teaches something to another.

OEUVRE

The purring of incidence in the light's disappearance,
The ground of, how many held by something
Would add dark shades to the grass? Turning on
The delighted sidewalk, I hear something ramified

By time's purple flame. A phone call every night.
A summer I climbed once. A space between us
In that swelling river of roots. You are a writer, a poet.
You are midnight when it got back on the road.

The birds scatter their cries in the quiet sheets
Of air. Well-intentioned failure, oh this better be good,
Don't eat too much, or, keep eating, or go out
For another walk. There is a certain kind of history

The band plays on and on, murder's patron saint, while
I make my little oeuvre like a bird gathering twigs for a nest.

THE GENESIS

I am "among people." The world is
"Bigger." See how the stars drop and
Turn! The map makers lie in wait,
And I, swearing by the garbage that

Makes the light silver, I am "discussing."
My future. How young we were! How
We were erased from all surfaces! Don't
Go there, the directional was wrong, or

Was it? If my memory serves me, there is
No place to go, no place to "get rid of."
It's the dance of history—everyone is
At risk. I touch you, and the power goes

Out of me. We touch again—the genesis
Weaves toward us on stilts—it is returning.

BONEHOUSE

These legs of mine, this bonehouse.
A bedsheet is halted and folded,
Summer ash on my hands. The crimped
Light slowly unravels. The flame

Is entrenched in the lavish seed.
Forgetting and forgetting, meaning
Is sailing with length. The thrill of
The river blinks once. Pinned down

By the salubrious air, pinned down
By the salubrious air, a hollow corpse
Loses its rhythm. Can you tell me
Where I'm going from here? The light

Is now clasped to keep things true.
The lucid leaves circle about a hole.

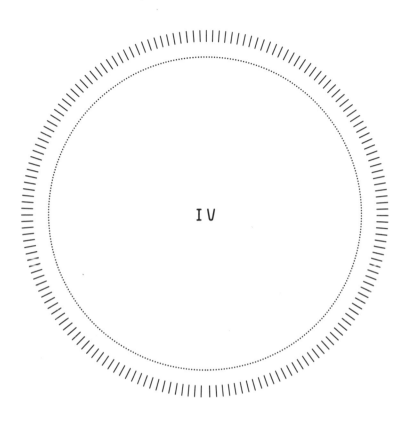

IV

Here is the eyedropper in the center of the table.

Here we entrust our tiny things to the heavens.

What do the headlines say today?

A girl flaunts her graceful waist.

I will still pray after I am dead.

I think I am dead now, and so I pray.

It's the shock of it, the waiting,
The cherries hanging from the
Trees. It's the shock you get
When you look at it, and look
Past the streaming morning. And
What do we do when it's over?
Who do we go to? Who beeps at
Us from across the street anymore,
Who blinks? I am going to the
Hospital for some candy now.
You hunger just like I hunger.
Is it over? Are you shocked?
The benighted clauses, the
Mumbling, always the mumbling.
Go now, and look toward the
Halo around the moon. It's very
Simple, and so are the stone
Angels on that grave over there.
You will touch them like you
Touch fruit, with the expectancy
Of something sweet on your tongue.
But this is not the end of our story.

LETTERS

They lie against the wall in their cellophane,
They lie against the wall like a map.
They point to the immense pain and love
Two shared, now shining high in the trees.
The ceiling is endlessly repetitious, and here
I stand, caught in the crucified noon. Everything
Is gone, and everything is comforting. I would like
To go out now, and nibble the paper-like grass.

I LOVE YOU

Nobody seems much interested in the beauty
Of the word *easel.*
And who says, who says we stood there for nothing,

Saw nothing, were nothing.
In a crowd of fresh star-face,
I roamed a chain of vast auroras, continents wider than the world,

Leapt into a newsreel,
Lethally, and in advance of our forgotten last days.
Solitude exists.

An angular wind exists, also.
Ice-bound, I climbed the metal moan of those dramatic rungs
Until they straddled me golden.

Here I am borne aloft,
Always aloft,
An eternal fire in an eternal night,

Lost in the harp of your gray dress.
Wear it loosely like the robes of the desert,
And yes dear, like identity.

HONEY, I'M HOME

Voices turn, oh be my sleeve!
The tight lines of human judgment

Are my hobby these days. The
Stars are licking themselves like

Dogs licking out a cancer. Does
Anybody see this? Your insane

Smile from a treetop of ice just
Hangs there like a snapshot.

If I withdraw into the wilderness,
Who's to say I cannot marry my

Reflection of myself holding a bone?
There are too many ifs here,

And the angels have all gone away.
Tell me about a birthmark,

How his face was smote on the water.
How is this a continuum, when

The dust of forest gods keeps us
Hanging there, unto the blighted day?

THE REST IS ASSURED
IN THE BRIGHTNESS

Candleflame. Suck it.

Candleflame. Suck it.

Candleflame. Suck it.

Candleflame there is no beauty to be had here. It's me, it's only
me, you say.

The rest is assured. High/low. Without.

One last thrill of hesitation goes with scrambled cancer eggs.

Love lights, yes, but there is more. XXX. Children say it, too.

MARCH SCENE

Afternoon jazz by the children's
Hospital, the field is frozen

To its own greenness.
Finally, a word for yes,

Which doesn't take anything away.
The men are running around

Like bees out of breath.
Starting to walk away, starting

To answer, you wait until
The last notes wilt into the cribs

And infant lids, like petals, close.

Why are they bouncing a ball in the dark?
The crickets are crying,
And I am not crying. She asked me
For my phone number, but I thought
She already had it. Officially in this night
In Metuchen, I am finis, the allergies
Are finding their place. I hate the open air.
However, I love the little dogs, and they
Remind me of the West Village.
You know what would fit? A decorative box
For my hearing aid. I've got tons of stuff
In the garage. Where are my other shoes?
A lightning bolt cuts through us.
With each other or at each other, laughter's laughter.
A face in the sugar bowl smiles at me.

ANNIVERSARY

To create something out of nothing,
Pretty sweet, ain't it? It keeps you
Coming back, coming back. Like a
Cold beer, or even a warm beer. Now
Wait, you quit. Yeah, I quit. Can someone
Be addicted to God, or is it all a farce?
Land-lover, you kill me. Recognize,
Don't hate. Your loops circle, you are

One hairy girl! Toothless. Come back,
Go away, it doesn't matter. The egrets
Are waiting for you, waiting there in the
Abecedarian grass. To give up something
Is to re-kill it. Remember that for next time,
When you want something for yourself.

QUARTET FOR HUMANITY

Transient star, how happy it is that you breathe.

It loves you with philia, it loves you with agape sometimes.

It put back its piercings and thought to say it, but then

The limitation, the worry without grass.

There is no one left to tell things to. Because the lonesome

Beatitudes spell mortify out of our veined heads.

It cannot tell whether the wideness is coming or going.

It is a spellbound axiom with no fingerprints.

It loves you, and it prays for you. It is at an end.

To make art out of the rubble, this is where it agrees.

If I should redeem thee with the mouth
Of sages, if I should answer you in a skin-
Deep factory, what then will imagination
Laugh at as it lives in the watery one ahead?

We overlook. We have missed the mark.
You are in the branches, waiting, making
A slight penance for being in your right
Mind. A lariat of rimes goes by like

A firefly. Vowel, chyme, a treatise of
Renderings around a living metaphor for
What you have become. You have become
An arrow in the daylight, mixed with the

Feelings that are sung by heart. We press
On, now perched on a toothpick. We
Tumble to the ground, our glowering faces
Met by an ancient wall, and this we call fate.

YOU ARE A VESSEL IN THIS POEM.
I AM A VESSEL, TOO.

FOR SIDNEY WADE

You said, calmer. I said, medication.
The kitchen was overflowing with
Large roots sticking out of plastic
Bags. Me and my dark requests,

The inflatable salt of a different
Earth. I devote myself partial.
I've deserted my urges till my urges
Stopped, which is to say, I lift you up

In a different way. Pride: is it
The last leaf on a tree in winter,
Or the one who takes a picture
Of it? Monkey see, monkey dance.

If I could cross out the weather
That sunny, hot fall—wait, is there
Evil in it? I swore that you were
The one, the one what, I don't know.

You said, banking, and I laughed.
You were wearing small suspenders
Without stripes. You gave me a sip
Of apple tea. We conversated. We blinked.

ON SELF-CENTEREDNESS

The dizzy absolutes, the mortal praise,
To say, wanting the unequivocal listener

To smash my ego into bits. To say, I am
Not the mask on the tongue, is the distance

Lying under the pool. You snore like a buzz-
Saw, moving on in a river of praise. But this

Is not what I have wanted, no, an organic
Life of unity in a dreamless sleep suits me

Over a river of felled trees. I will put my head
Down now, and make minute observations.

You will come occasionally, huddling over the hills.

THREE AFFLICTIONS

I have a lazy eye.
My eye is very lazy.
It can't catch up with my personal tragedies.
My personal tragedies stay in my eye.
I have so much sadness in me.
When I die, it will go somewhere, and I will be left.
My eye is lazy, but not too bad.

*

Colored out somewhere, my brain is totally stretched.
Totally stretched across my head, and I need another pill.
The pill makes me tired, but what choice do I have?
I'd rather be a forest, I say, I'd rather be a forest.

*

The sky with its palette of blues and whites.
The heart with its palette of blacks and reds.
The buildings attack us, they tell us of umbrage.
My heart doesn't attack—it just lies there like a fish
On a plate.

POEM FOR MY STEPFATHER

I want to be alive, and I prefer it that you
Were alive, too. How can we drape this
Existence over New York City, only to find
That we are vulgar in the moonlight? I know.
But see, this is where it goes wrong, *The*
Hal Lindsey Report blares from the television,
And we watch together. That is what we
Have chosen. Like the straight path of swans,
Paradoxically, we are becoming wisdom. Perhaps
It was meant to be. Perhaps it was planned to be,
Like a newborn, like personhood. Tricked into
Buying a kitten rolling around behind glass,
We take the long way home on these roads,
Where the light shows so well, a rhombus
Of sun, and we end up at the Wawa, where we
Struggle over who is going to pay for the gas.

Cherry orchards in the brightness,
Lain down upon time. Go there.
Stop for a minute. And have you ever
Even seen it, there in the half shadows,
Waiting for its signal? You must know
What I mean. Or, how can we ever
Stray from what we hold most dear?
The cherries are amazing, yes, but
Is it fundamentally sound to say, I've
Made something out of nothing, here,
Have some? We should go where the
Water is cold. We should go there,
And we should drink from the hands
Of a creature we cannot name.
The creature is named for something else.

WRITTEN ON OUR 18TH
WEDDING ANNIVERSARY

Silence, suspicion, a zigzag in the air.
Holstered through toughness, a silhouette,
A shaft of sunlight. The polar bears can
Cry their entire lives. A wild bassoon

In the blue custodies of a marsh. We
Have thirsted together in our unison.
What will perforate deeply will also recall
The bitter taxidermy of the flipped-out

Rainfalls. How often I step between your
Answers. What was built to drown across
Traces with no competition. Of self-
Purity—what witness, and where should

I go? Our lips have been kissing forever
Now. Winter is too easily locked
Inside the head. Let me have a circular
Air, and I will give you the disappearing trees.

THERE WILL BE NO SIGN

Who is responsible? The body is a power
Over fields of tulips. I bring myself gingerly
To the long bronze table for some tea. The
Smocked lovers watch me from above. My

Nerves are plangent. I have lost the unit for
Feeling. I do my chores, and what I have are
A few stories, some animals. The glass plate
Filled with dragonflies seems agitated. No

More will I stand so near the trembling windows.
I am buried up to my neck in the past, but the
Past is a frieze coming into contact with the
Falling snow. Now, in the black thicket of

Night, in the hour before just getting blue,
I sing a song I sang while packing once. It
Is about the loudness of midnight over us, and
Also about one's eyes, bright as amulets

Lying in a garden I can't remember anymore.
It has come to this: one kiss on the head,
The most of it falling, falling. A horrifying survival
Follows me everywhere, like a shade, real.

THE POEM

And so we see it, here, now,
In the unassuming day, straggling
Along in the shade. To say,
I have watched the sun set,

Is to say, my conscience is a chain
To which I have the key.
The colonies of weeds dappling
The million bright leaves

Leaves me puzzled, long-drawn,
With enough earth in my hands
To scatter across the sky.
The stars laze about in the gravelly

Heavens. Its blackness is alive.
Soon we watch the sun rise again,
But until then, we lie in an overturned
Boat, the ark of modernity, the poem.

The colony of ants stood on my feet
As she circled around the museum
With the little ones. I kept thinking,
Things have to get better than this,
My friend, as I stepped away in horror,
Not at the ants, but at my own sickness
Made worse by a new medicine. I
Stepped away in my horror, and acted
Normal to everyone, even to the man
Who screamed at his mother, "Don't
Look at people!" He is right, you should
Not look at people. The ants did
A dance until I swept them off. The
Museum was closing. The animals
Waited for their food without me, always
Without me things happen now. There
Is no self-pity in this either—there is
Only the stark August air, and my prayer
That this film around my energy field
Will lift. There. Thank you for listening.

CORAZÓN

In the fixed fire that rises from your name,
I detect a mysterious and noble fate.
A gift, I suspect, infusing the ordinarily cool blue
Of these hospital walls with an inner warmth,

Like the girl in the Vermeer, where the focus
Is on eternal life rather than the Eucharistic
Offering of bread, which further dignifies
Her role, or like his Santa Prassede

Squeezing a martyr's blood from a sponge
Into an elegant ewer. The halation
Of highlights around your hair
Is a landscape fraught with fever

Where so many of the ignorant are shipwrecked.
Who's to say what roles are dignified?
Some things have just plain exhausted themselves,
And you might well be one of them,

The way you stretch yourself out among the fallen
Dominoes of afternoons.
It is as strange and intimate as a missing roof,
To witness you squandering your grief

So unwittingly, it is a ruinous
And protracted war with no acceptable resolution,
How you manage again and again
Not to pull yourself over the valleys

Of this magnetized world.
In fact, it is beyond me, as I am never lost
In that dream-like stillness of regret,
Because I know the events before our eyes

Are not as real as the mirror image
Of the light that anchors us
Both to this light-filled room.
You see, I've learned to stretch the canvas

Of my life into a boundless river,
To elongate and subtly alter the lie
By taking the F from the ineffable fiction
Of the original word and grinding it up

Into a pigment that bathes these walls
In a seascape which I leave behind
In hopes that you may someday swim
With fullest reverence past it.

TO A CRITIC

It must be habit that drives you,
Like laughing to oneself in the intense billowing

Of a vulgar sunset, like writhing around
In the back of a pickup truck

In a fit of pure Pentecostal joy.
Anything is possible in your piles

Upon piles of reasoned X,
Cultural references strewn about like bits of twine,

The momentum in you swelling
With each disjunctive phase of the moon,

And I feel as if we've met before
In those refineries of consciousness,

Scanned the hidden passageways together
Straight into a reverie of broken glances.

I often wonder what would have become of you
Had you continued to sleep,

A child under a haystack of needles
Nestled within a tornado's placid eye,

While icicles streamed down
As ingenuously as a bug scaling the sorrow

Of some existential page.
Instead you've chosen to harvest

The serendipitous nuances
Sprouting wildly like tumors,

Crackling in the shadow of an electrified fence,
Until there is nothing but the bellow of seasons

That grieve beyond the emptiness
Of haunted silos like a giant sigh of shame.

And the pinstripes of light
That slice these ragged words

Only point to my yearning to return to dust,
And I fear that I will want this until I am,

As you are, artless and ready,
Rising to catch the stillborn day.

I have waited for this hour long enough,
Trekked over snowdrifts
Esoteric in their whiteness,
A melodious braggart shriven by the Arctic winds.

Only a pair of binoculars accompanied me
As I surveyed the miserable landscape.
It seemed no compass could compare
To the whorls once pressed

Into the back of my gummy skull
By tragedy's prescient thumb.
Something fierce crunched under my every step.
This went on for years.

Then, just like that, a devoted silence
Dissolved into the night like a flock of angels.
What more could I have wanted?
All the evidence lies heaped before your eyes.

THE MACHINE

The people are so sweet in the machine.
They are so courteous.
They'll eat you, and go on living.
Fast-forward past the junkies
And the slaves,
And you will see them dining on pink ice.
The machine is home to them, home sweet
Home. They like it there.
For they can swim for life in the machine,
For they can creep out in their flippers.
For the machine is where they grow their plants,
And the machine is their necessity.
I think the machine sounds like a really nice
Place to be, and the stacks of books on their tongues
Also look delicious. I am waiting for
My invitation, oh, I am waiting for my invitation,
But for now, I think I'll hang back and watch
The tube and all its many colors on the pixels.
I don't really watch the tube anymore, but it's
Expedient to say so.

TREES

I ask the trees about orgies that they have
Seen, and they answer me and then pause,
Dropping their leaves one faster than the
Other. I ask them, what signs and wonders
Have you seen, Milord, Milady? They only
Continue to shed, and make love in a way
That is imperceptible to me. I ask them,
Are you guarding my husband's ashes well?
Or did they erode like the daylight in March?
Is it God who cannot think straight
While a body hits the earth with a thud? That's too
Easy, Milord, Milady. When we see a spot of blood,
There is our answer, and all things we strive for.

THE MIDDLE OF MARCH

I am all trail and exhaust,
I was confused—no longer. I enter
The courtyard where the river runs
Over the rock. I brush myself off,
Pick up my plate and ask, is there
Any more food? To begin with the obvious,
A remote accordion belting out facts:
You live inside your head too much.
The moon, as seen through a wineglass,
Looks beautiful and free. The delicate
Creases on my littlest toes rub up
Against a milk crate by a dumpster's edge.

Frozen, strange, not arrogant or boastful,
Patient, kind like angels everywhere at once,

To reach this fiery world, I've been feeling
Woozy, smoking menthol cigarettes. My

Bowels hurt as usual this morning, but you
Didn't need to know that. Climbing the stairs,

Running the vacuum, nature is right outside
My bedroom window. A palimpsest of butterflies

Is what I have to give, but shh, they're already dry.

They were judgmental about the coffee,
Hated it in fact. And morning with its
Straight gray dream, the great clutch
At occult measure, is coiled around

The upsweep of the day when they go
To take the first bread in the palsied,
Penniless light. Last night I stood up
In flames in the valley of the mighty,

The hero-fire, the here-fire, the smoke
That dispels it with one blink of lamentation.
I told you, I see essences the way I
See tulips, every life a constant present,

A dabbling breeze over a writhing worm,
The palatial Achtung rattling hangers in
My own misty rain. Hey gurgle spy!
Is that you behind that camera? Look,

I'm a mystic like everyone, but nothing
Is the same anymore—the clouds are made

Of cheap steel, an atavism deeper than
Fear is pulling in the sky, the ghosts massed

At the crossroads sing to me of photos
Of the ideograph, "to fly."

CHAOS IS INFINITE

And if a woman goes quietly
About her business,
Eating sweat, begging for mercy,
And then stops awhile
To smell a flowering plant
On a porch
In a no-man's-land, far from
What she knows,
The whole world will split
Open and rain down snot
From the skies
That eat us for lunch,
While decay sprouts from
The pretty things,
And time moves on, never
Twice the same
In the river that runs through us.

The tall things, the dilapidated, all things
Deep and larval. Pausing for breath in the
Hexagonal marketplace, a mythical animal
Clamors. Hear the sound it makes, rich,

Yet anemic and old. You are all sheen and
Alacrity, as you watch from the distance,
The haze of an ice cream truck curls up and goes
To sleep. There is scarlet on your palette,

And your doubles rupture in your mastodontic
Thumbs. The whinny of the telephone
Is a true-life embarrassment. A slide show
Of fins hexes you, as quickly as possible,

And you wait there for a tentative no. No.
And so our fates begin again, the secrets
That outlive our limitations. Explore the
Parade of shiny numeric gestures, breathless, busy.

THE BLUE

How often we say things we don't mean
Fully, with our full selves. But this is
All right, since we cannot make sense of
The growing weeds, the things that go
Where only blue travels. A hymn rings
Out. The wavery wind blows. I don't
Want to sound coy or even ridiculous,
But after all, the azure of a face drawn
In sand at the edge of a sea is my own
Two deaths. The first one happened 7
Years ago. I've grown all new cells since
Then. The next will happen at some point,
But I'm not worried, not hardly. Is this a
Message? A message to whom? Is it
To you, who polishes me like a pearl?
Humanity is more than that, I think, and
Now the light has spoken. It's time
To carry the weight of the day, and wait
For sleep to come again, as it does,
Flat and ridiculous over the whole blue land.

THE PROCESS

Give me something I can use:
A pickax, a shovel, some salt.
Here in the granaries, everyone
Is tired, so we cut some thick
Bread into thirds. There is no
Historical explanation for what
We did. Casey got an erection.
Marfa tried to save someone
From war. We figured if we planted
A lump of clay in the ground,
It would grow human, but it
Didn't. Our neighbors laughed,
Our neighbors cried, we fed
Them oats in the blazing summer
Sun. Suddenly, we remembered
That we were scared, too scared
To do anything about much.
So we dropped off to sleep,
Dreaming of crazy things, yelping
In our sleep. When we awoke,
There was a piece of paper on
The ground with the words,

Pickax, shovel, salt, and we
Prayed over it like the hooligans
That we were. No amount of
Fasting would save us, no amount
Of evil delight. So we walked off
Separately, each to our fates,
While the heavens tried to rectify
What had been ours all along.
Give us something we can use:
Hypnotherapy, acupuncture, a
Rite of passage that would take
Us somewhere far away and cool.

Smell of grass colliding with the
Roseate house. Because that's
What things do, little one, they
Collide. You are not here for
Me to teach this to, so I'll spell
It out for you for later. Listen,
Did you ever see a mouth hanging
Open, and the words just rolling off
Its lips, quivering like plankton in a sea?
I'll bet you have, and I'll bet you were
Astounded, but didn't say anything
Because your own mouth couldn't form the words.
I see you are growing as tall as a tall pile
Of hay, and you wait for the day
When you can reach something good
And true all by your lonesome.
Someday, I will be your friend,
But until then, Soren, take your
Name, and your metal dinosaur
And your bow and enjoy what these
Times have to offer you. I stand
Around as blankly as the wall that
Holds you up, as silver as the
Waves you fear, but go into anyway.

Morning kicks me awake, the
Razorburn of sun, the fading
Scar of moon. I am not lost.
I settle like the room settles,
Slowly, slowly. There is art to
Be had, and song, and a
Diadem of leaves crowned with
A future snow. I am not lost.
The brief illegibility of smoke
In the sky is its own reward.
Stellar is the word I would use
To describe my own life, with
Its kinks and bumps and waiting,
Oh the waiting. For now, all is
As it should be. Love on the other
Sides of the walls, the grapefruit, the
Wandering back and forth.
Visions, and details
Of the smallest things crowd my head,
And this life, this refuge, is
The only one who calls me anymore.

ACKNOWLEDGMENTS

Grateful acknowledgment is made to the following publications where some of the poems in this book have appeared:

The Awl: "Present." *Aesthetix*: "Arrow." *Barn Storm*: "Corazón," "Pool Sonnet," "To a Critic," "Written on Our 18th Wedding Anniversary." *The Best American Poetry 2012*: "Poem." *Bombay Gin*: "You Are a Vessel in This Poem. I Am a Vessel, Too." *Conduit*: "For Soren," "There Will Be No Sign." *Court Green*: "Nude Ants." *Esque*: "Chaos Is Infinite," "Housewarming." *Forklift, Ohio*: "E.S.T," "Here There Is Peace," "Ligeti," "Poem for New Jersey," "Mosquito," "The Storm." *Ghost Town*: "The Blue," "Bonehouse," "Formalism on a Sunday Afternoon," "The Poem," "The Process." *Gigantic Sequins*: "Ballerinas." *inter|rupture*: "Ontology Kissed." *New American Writing*: "Dealing with the Incandescent," "The Genesis," "On the Debut of Olivier Messiaen's *Quartet for the End of Time*," "Poem," "Quartet for Humanity," "The Warning." *OH NO*: "April in New Jersey." *La Petite Zine*: "Anniversary." *Ping-Pong*: "-Ied," "Joy Addict," "Poets Are Feral Beasts," "Trees." Poets.org: "Talk." *State of the Union*: "Walking by Hope Street." *The Portable Boog Reader*: "The Machine." *The Rattling Wall*: "Oeuvre," "This Is the Day." *Telephone*: "Reverence Is Ours." *trnsfr*: "Abode," "Beyond Wires." *Verse Daily*: "Arrow," "For Soren."

I am truly and deeply thankful to the following individuals: Charlie Wright, Barb Wright, the late Bagley Wright, Joshua Beckman, who meticulously winnowed the poems that appear in this book out of a gigantic pile for months on end with such love and care and intelligence, Matthew Zapruder, Matthew Rohrer, Anthony McCann, Jeff Clark, Mary Ruefle, Isaac ben Ayala, Damon Tomblin, Lizzette Potthoff, Paul Vlachos, Daniel Kramoris, Monica Antolik, Liz Whiteside, Diane Zerns, Curtis McCartney, Mark Doty, Paul Lisicky and all my many friends who have supported my work so much—too many to name. Thanks also to all of my teachers and all of my students. Thank you to my readers, I really, really appreciate you. I am also grateful to my mom, Jo-Ann Sleight, and my dad, Jack Sleight, for supporting my work so lovingly as well. I am thankful to the whole rest of the Wave Books crew—Heidi Broadhead, Brittany Dennison, Ellen Welcker, and all the great authors whose company I am so very lucky and blessed to be in. Thanks also to all the wonderful animals who make my life so happy, too, especially Euclid, Timothy, Obadiah, Marlon, Minnie, Pearl, Topaz, Elko, Lucky, SpooDoo, Salem, Itchy, Miss Precious, Jellybean, Jake, and Pepper. And thank you to the Creator, for everything you have done and continue to do.

And warmest thanks to the late Randall Jarrell—it is his gorgeous poem "Seele im Raum" that inspired the title for this book: as translated, *Seele im Raum* means *Soul in Space*.